DISASTER SEARCH DOGS

by Melissa McDaniel

Consultant: Wilma Melville, Founder
National Disaster Search Dog Foundation

BEARPORT
PUBLISHING COMPANY, INC.

New York, New York

Special thanks to Wilma Melville who founded the:
National Disaster Search Dog Foundation
206 N. Signal Street, Suite R
Ojai, CA 93023
(888) 4K9-HERO
www.SearchDogFoundation.org

The Search Dog Foundation is a not-for-profit organization that rescues dogs, gives them professional training, and partners them with firefighters to find people buried alive in disasters. They produce the most highly trained search dogs in the nation.

Design and production by Dawn Beard Creative and Octavo Design and Production, Inc.

Credits

Library of Congress Cataloging-in-Publication Data

McDaniel, Melissa.
   Disaster search dogs / by Melissa McDaniel; consultant, Wilma Melville.
      p. cm.—(Dog heroes)
   Includes bibliographical references (p.   ) and index.
   ISBN 1-59716-012-1 (lib. bdg.)   ISBN 1-59716-035-0 (pbk.)
   1. Search dogs—Juvenile literature. 2. Rescue dogs—Juvenile literature.
   3. Disasters—Juvenile literature. I. Melville, Wilma. II. Title. III. Series.

SF428.73.M39 2005
636.7'0886—dc22

                        2004020748

For more information, write to Bearport Publishing Company, Inc., 101 Fifth Avenue, Suite 6R, New York, New York 10003. Printed in the United States of America.

1 2 3 4 5 6 7 8 9 10

Table of Contents

It's an Earthquake!

September 19, 1985, was a foggy morning in Mexico City, the largest city in Mexico. People and cars rushed through the streets. Suddenly, the ground **trembled** and began to shake. Walls tumbled and buildings fell to the ground. People screamed and sirens sounded. An **earthquake** was beginning.

Large parts of Mexico City had been destroyed by the time the ground stopped shaking. More than 3,500 buildings were badly damaged or had fallen. Almost 10,000 people had died. Many other people were trapped under the **rubble**. **Rescuers** rushed to find them. There was no time to lose.

There are about 8,000 earthquakes every day around the world. Most of them are small and do no damage.

To the Rescue in Mexico City

One of the rescuers, named Aly, was a **disaster** search dog. He looked for people buried at the site by searching for their **scent**.

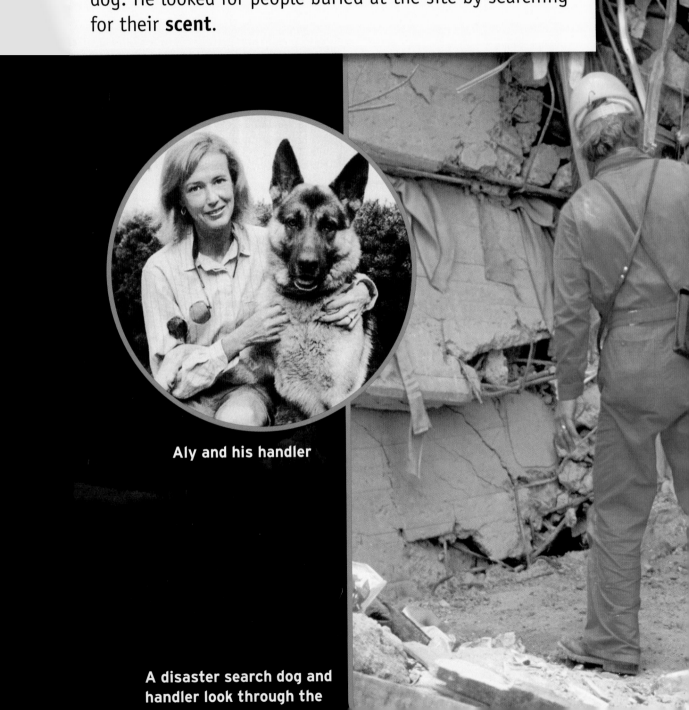

Aly and his handler

A disaster search dog and handler look through the

Aly worked his way through the rubble. Suddenly, he stopped and touched a pile of rocks. Then he pointed his nose and began to bark. That was the signal! Aly smelled someone. He was showing his **handler** where the scent was the strongest.

Rescuers began looking for people where Aly had pointed his nose. They found two women who could hardly breathe. Aly had helped save their lives.

Most people buried under buildings can live for three days without water.

The Nose Knows

When people are buried in a fallen building, disaster search dogs come to the rescue. They look for people after a **hurricane** hits. They search for people lost during **floods**. Dogs are better searchers than people because they have a better sense of smell.

A dog's sense of smell is 1,000 times better than a person's sense of smell.

All people give off a scent. The scent floats in the air. Disaster search dogs use their strong noses to pick up this scent through the rubble. It would take a team of 30 people all day to search a small building that has fallen. One disaster dog can search it in two hours or less.

Ready to Help

Dogs have been used to find lost people for a long time. More than 300 years ago in Europe, Saint Bernards searched for people lost in **snowstorms**.

In the United States, police dogs searched for people in fallen buildings. These dogs, however, were not trained to work in disasters.

In the 1970s, trainers began teaching dogs to look for people after a disaster. The U.S. government started a group called the Federal Emergency Management Agency, or FEMA. This group deals with disasters. Many dogs with lots of training become part of FEMA's rescue teams.

Saint Bernards look for people lost in the snow in the Swiss Alps in 1955.

England, a country in Europe, was bombed a lot during World War II (1939–1945). Dogs were used to find people trapped in the rubble of the buildings that fell.

The Best Breeds

Many **breeds** of dog can become disaster search dogs. Some trainers like to work with small dogs. They can easily fit into tight spaces where people might be trapped. Other trainers think large dogs work best. They can move more quickly over piles of rubble.

Kinzi is a member of the Salt Lake Search and Rescue team.

Disaster search dogs need to be strong. They must like to hunt and find things. They need to be able to work near loud noises. These dogs should also be willing to do things other dogs would not do, such as climb a ladder.

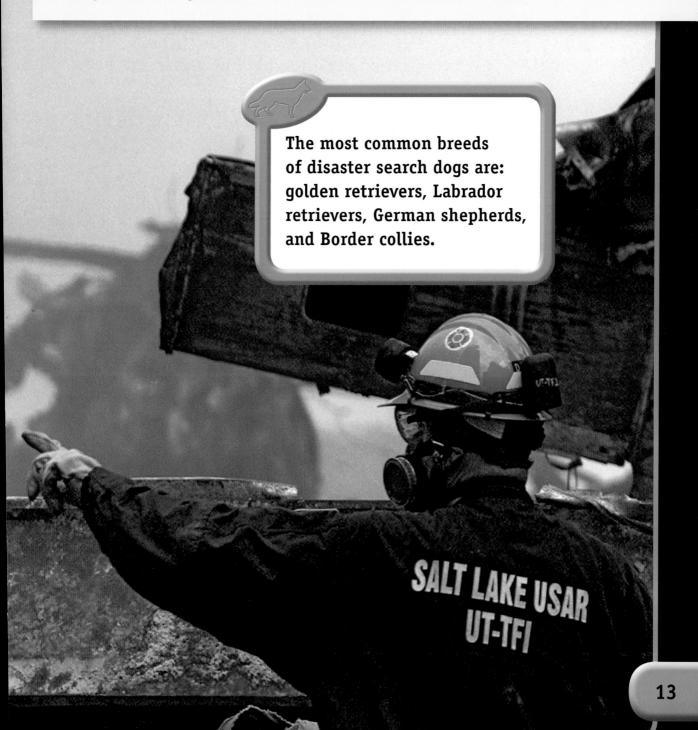

The most common breeds of disaster search dogs are: golden retrievers, Labrador retrievers, German shepherds, and Border collies.

On the Go

The dogs that make good disaster search dogs don't always make the best pets. Some puppies want to play all day. Often people don't want puppies that are too playful. These puppies often end up at an animal **shelter**.

Many puppies that are rescued from the shelters become disaster search dogs. Since disaster search animals work 12 hours at a time, a lively puppy is just what is needed.

Disaster search dogs live with their handlers. These people train the puppies. The training begins between the ages of 8 and 18 months.

Alex plays with some lively puppies.

About one out of six disaster search dog handlers are part of the police or fire departments. The rest are people who have other jobs.

It's a Game

Handlers train disaster search dogs to find buried people. How? The handler pretends to be the missing person. He or she runs away and hides. The dog races off and finds the handler. The dog is then rewarded with a game of tug. The dog is learning that finding people is fun.

Soon, the dog learns to find people he doesn't know. Whenever the dog finds a hidden person, he's rewarded. With practice, the dog can find someone buried under 20 feet of rubble. Most disaster dogs are trained to bark for 30 seconds or more when they find someone.

Lee Prentiss and his disaster search dog Tara look for a victim during a training exercise.

Some disaster search dogs are also trained to find dead bodies. The dogs learn to give a different signal for a dead body than for a live person.

17

Training for Safety

Disaster search dogs are also taught how to make their way through fallen buildings. This lesson takes lots of practice. The dogs spend time climbing up and down ladders. They walk across narrow boards. They learn how to squeeze through pipes and move over piles of rocks.

Disaster search dogs keep from getting hurt because they're quick and strong. They're trained to stay away from broken glass and sharp pieces of metal.

After two years, the dogs are highly trained. They're ready to work in a real disaster.

Many disaster search dogs also train on a seesaw.

Springing into Action

Disaster search dogs came to the rescue after **tornadoes** tore through Oklahoma in 1999. That same year, Hurricane Floyd blew across North Carolina. Disaster search dogs looked for people trapped in houses and flooded towns.

On April 19, 1995, a government building was blown up in Oklahoma City, Oklahoma. There were 168 people killed. More than 500 people were hurt. Only one person trapped in the rubble was alive. A disaster search dog found this person.

Firefighters and a disaster search dog look through the rubble of the building that was blown up in Oklahoma City.

There is now a museum in the place where the building in Oklahoma once stood.

A Terrible Time

The world was shocked. **Terrorists** had crashed airplanes into the World Trade Center in New York City. Within hours, the two towers fell to the ground.

Thousands of people had been inside. Was anyone alive? Disaster search dogs and their handlers came from all over the country. They helped search for people. For days, the dogs looked through rubble. Only one dog found anyone alive. If more people had lived through the disaster, the dogs would have found them, too.

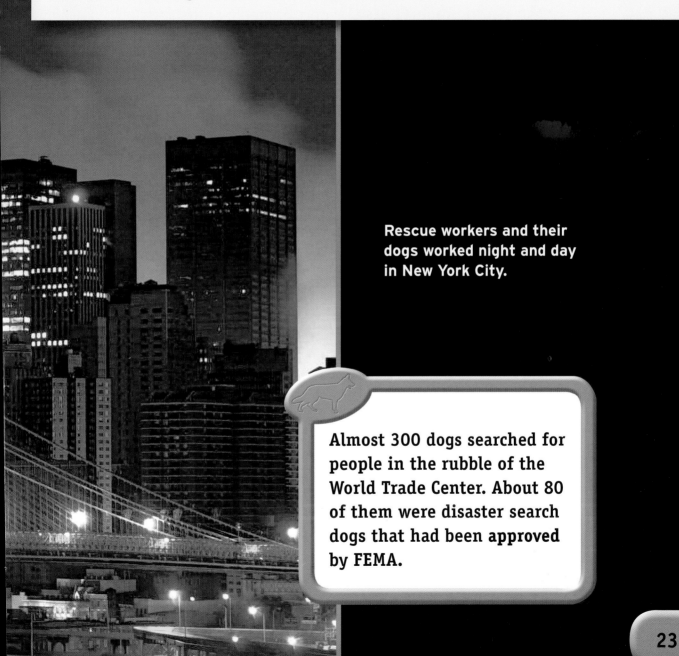

Rescue workers and their dogs worked night and day in New York City.

Almost 300 dogs searched for people in the rubble of the World Trade Center. About 80 of them were disaster search dogs that had been **approved** by FEMA.

Danger on the Job

Disaster search dogs face danger everyday. Some get cuts or burns on their paws. It's the handler's job to keep the dog safe.

At the World Trade Center, a dog named Servus fell into a hole. The hole was full of ash and dust. When he was pulled out, Servus couldn't breathe. He was taken to an animal hospital. Doctors worked hard. Soon Servus was breathing again.

Coach, another disaster search dog at the World Trade Center, gets some help at a care center.

Later, Servus and his handler returned to the fallen towers. Servus leaped out of the car. His handler told him to stay inside. Servus, however, refused. Dog and human went back to work.

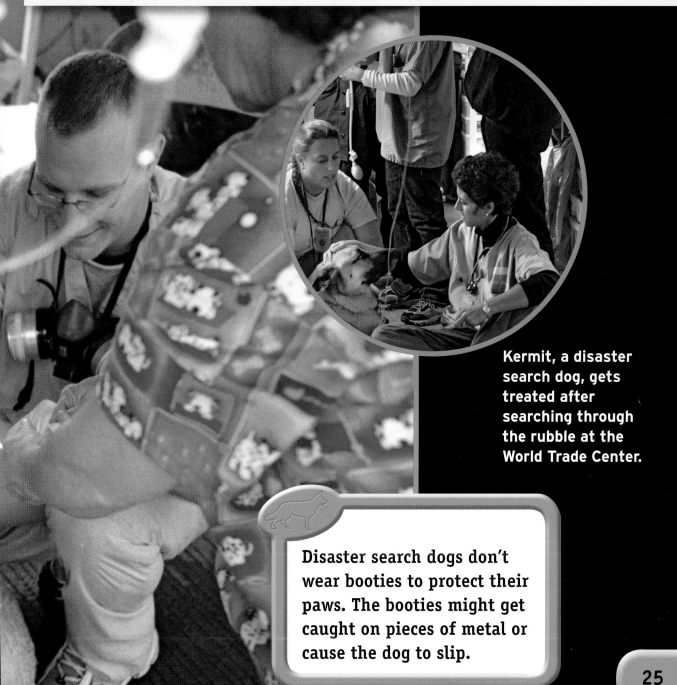

Kermit, a disaster search dog, gets treated after searching through the rubble at the World Trade Center.

Disaster search dogs don't wear booties to protect their paws. The booties might get caught on pieces of metal or cause the dog to slip.

Dog Heroes

Disasters can happen at any time. No one knows when an earthquake or a tornado will hit. Disaster search dogs, however, are always ready to lend a helping paw.

In one test, it took a person two hours to find someone hidden in a fallen building. A disaster search dog found the person in five minutes.

Disaster search dogs are better than any machine at finding people. They are heroes who don't ask for big rewards. All they want is to play a game of tug and hear their handler say, "Good dog."

A search team after a tornado hit Oklahoma in 1999

Just the Facts

- A dog can smell a person from a mile away.

- Disaster search dogs can be male or female.

- A disaster search dog found two people alive after the 1985 Mexico City earthquake. They were trapped inside a car. The car was in a parking garage that had fallen.

- Bear was the first rescue dog to arrive at the World Trade Center on September 11, 2001. He was the only dog to find anyone alive.

- In 1986, an earthquake hit El Salvador, a country in Central America. In less than two days, four disaster search dogs saved seven people.

Border collie

golden retriever

German shepherd

Labrador retriever

Glossary

approved (uh-PROOVD) officially accepted by someone or something

breeds (BREEDZ) types of a certain animal

disaster (duh-ZASS-tur) a sudden event causing much damage, loss, or suffering

earthquake (URTH-*kwayk*) a sudden shaking of a part of the earth, caused by movement of the earth's crust

floods (FLUHDZ) overflows of water onto land that is not normally underwater

handler (HAND-lur) someone who trains and works with animals

hurricane (HUR-uh-*kane*) a violent storm with very high winds

rescuers (RESS-kyoo-urz) people or animals who save someone who is in danger

rubble (RUHB-uhl) pieces of broken rocks and bricks

scent (SENT) the smell of an animal or person

shelter (SHEL-tur) a place where an animal that is not wanted can stay

snowstorms (SNOH-*stormz*) storms with strong winds and heavy snow

terrorists (TER-ur-ists) people who use violence and threats to achieve their goals

tornadoes (tor-NAY-dohz) violent, whirling columns of air that are cone–shaped clouds and move quickly over land

trembled (TREM-buhld) shook

Bibliography

Bidner, Jen. *Dog Heroes: Saving Lives and Protecting America.* Guilford, CT: Lyons Press (2002).

Glen, Samantha, and Mary Pesaresi. *Search and Rescue.* New York, NY: Ballantine Books (1997).

Gorrell, Gena K. *Working Like a Dog: The Story of Working Dogs through History.* Toronto, Canada: Tundra Books (2003).

Singer, Marilyn. *A Dog's Gotta Do What a Dog's Gotta Do.* New York, NY: Henry Holt (2000).

Weisbord, Merrily, and Kim Kachanoff. *Dogs With Jobs: Working Dogs Around the World.* New York, NY: Pocket Books (2000).

Whittemore, Hank, and Caroline Hebard. *So That Others May Live.* New York, NY: Bantam (1995).

Read More

Clutton-Brock, Juliet. *Dog.* New York, NY: Alfred A. Knopf (1991).

Jackson, Donna M. *Hero Dogs: Courageous Canines in Action.* New York, NY: Little, Brown and Company (2003).

Mattern, Joanne. *They Too Were Heroes: True Tales of Courageous Dogs.* Mahwah, NJ: Troll Communications (2003).

Presnall, Judith Janda. *Rescue Dogs.* San Diego, CA: KidHaven Press (2002).

Learn More Online

Visit these Web sites to learn more about disaster search dogs:

www.bearsearchandrescue.org

www.disasterdog.org

www.fema.gov/usr/usr_canines

www.SearchDogFoundation.org

Index

About the Author

Melissa McDaniel is a writer and editor who lives in New York City.
She is the author of 20 books for young people.